Rice Co

Recipes

A Complete Cookbook

BY: Valeria Ray

License Notes

A Special Reward for Purchasing My Book!

Thank you, cherished reader, for purchasing my book and taking the time to read it. As a special reward for your decision, I would like to offer a gift of free and discounted books directly to your inbox. All you need to do is fill in the box below with your email address and name to start getting amazing offers in the comfort of your own home. You will never miss an offer because a reminder will be sent to you. Never miss a deal and get great deals without having to leave the house! Subscribe now and start saving!

https://valeria-ray.gr8.com

Contents

Delicious Rice Cooker Recipes

MMMMMMMMMMMMMMMMMMMMMMMMMMMMMMMMMMMMM

(1) Steamed Tofu & Asparagus

Rice cookers work in much the same way as steamers, so it's not rocket science that this tofu and veggie steamer blend can be cooked perfectly in a rice cooker. It's like a tasty stir-fry without any added fat.

Yield: 4 Servings

Preparation Time: 35 minutes

List of Ingredients:

- 1 tablespoon of shoyu
- 1 minced garlic clove
- ½ peeled & sliced carrot, small
- 6 ounces of cubed tofu, fried
- ½ of a small bunch of chopped asparagus
- 1 teaspoon each of honey, mirin, sesame seed oil and vegetable oil

MMMMMMMMMMMMMMMMMMMMMMMMMMMMMMMMMMMM

Methods:

1. Toss all ingredients together in mixing bowl. Transfer on to an oven-safe plate.

2. Place In the rice cooker and steam for 15 to 20 minutes. Remove and serve.

We can't leave out a few great desserts you can make in a rice cooker…

(2) Spanish Rice

Spanish rice is a wonderful side for Mexican inspired dishes. This recipe is the ultimate in "easy", since the rice cooker does the work. Just dump in the ingredients and it'll do the rest. It will allow you to stretch your Mexican meals out, and give you leftovers for bean burritos the next day.

Yield: 5 Servings

Preparation Time: 40 minutes

List of Ingredients:

- 1 to 3 tablespoons of chili powder
- 3 cubes bouillon
- 1 diced onion, small
- 3 & ½ cups of water, filtered
- 1 x 14-oz. can of tomatoes, diced, with the juice
- 2 cups of rice
- 1 teaspoon of cumin
- ½ teaspoons of garlic powder
- ¾ teaspoons of salt, kosher

MMMMMMMMMMMMMMMMMMMMMMMMMMMMMMMMMMMMM

Methods:

1. Place rice in rice cooker bottom. Add water and tomatoes.

2. Add spices and onion. Stir a bit to dissolve spices. Cook using manufacturer directions.

3. After rice has cooked, add salt as desired. Serve in tacos or burritos or as a great side dish.

(3) Lime Cilantro Rice

This is an easy to make copycat recipe from a well-known Southwestern style restaurant in the United States. It will liven up your plain rice with cilantro and lime juice. It can be used as a yummy side dish or you can top it with salsa and cooked veggies to make a burrito bowl. Your Japanese rice cooker will do the bulk of the work for you.

Yield: 4 Servings

Preparation Time: 35 minutes

List of Ingredients:

- 2 cups of white rice, long grain, washed
- 1-2 teaspoons of oil, olive
- 1 lime, zest and ½ juice only
- 2 tablespoons of fresh cilantro, minced
- 1 teaspoon of salt, kosher

MMMMMMMMMMMMMMMMMMMMMMMMMMMMMMMMMMMMM

Methods:

1. Heat skillet on med-low. Add rice and oil. Stir & toast for five to eight minutes. Rice should be aromatic and golden in color.

2. Place salt and toasted rice in the rice cooker. Follow the manufacturer's instructions as to appropriate waterline to use. Close lid. Set on Cook.

3. After rice cooks, open rice cooker. Fluff with fork. Transfer to bowl. Add lime juice and zest plus cilantro. Serve.

(4) Fat & Fluffy Japanese Pancakes

This is a huuuuge pancake, and you can use your rice cooker to make one. You don't have to stand at the stove, flipping pancakes. Just add the batter and allow your rice cooker to do all the work.

Yield: 2 Servings

Preparation Time: 60 minutes

List of Ingredients:

- 1 & ½ cups of milk, low fat
- 2 eggs, large
- 2 tablespoons of sugar, granulated
- 2 & ½ teaspoons of baking powder
- 2 cups of flour, all-purpose

MMMMMMMMMMMMMMMMMMMMMMMMMMMMMMMMMMMMM

Methods:

1. Whisk milk and eggs together in large bowl until blended well. Add the rest of the ingredients. Whisk until any lumps that remain are small.

2. Grease interior of rice cooker pot. Pour batter in. Close.

3. Set on Cook for 45 mins. When finished, cake will pull slightly away from edges. It should bounce back and feel firm.

4. Allow pancake to cool for several minutes. Invert cake on a plate. Surface should be brown. Serve with syrup or powdered sugar.

(5) Fudge Lava Cake

You may not be sure that your rice cooker can handle this lava cake, but I'm assuring you that it can. You have to be patient, to be sure. It may take two hours or so for the cake to be fully cooked, depending on the power level of your rice cooker. Start this cake before you begin to cook the meal that will precede it. When you check, if it still seems too liquid-y, just let it cook longer. When it IS done, it's a moist and delicious cake that you'll never forget.

Yield: 6-8 Servings

Preparation Time: 1 hour to 2 hours & 20 minutes

List of Ingredients:

- 1 box chocolate cake mix – mixed by instructions on box
- 1 can ready to use frosting, chocolate

MMMMMMMMMMMMMMMMMMMMMMMMMMMMMMMMMMMMM

Methods:

1. Place ingredients in bowl of rice cooker. Spoon in ½ of frosting in middle of cake batter.

2. Place bowl in rice cooker. Push Cook. If set on Slow Cook, it may take up to two hours. Check on it until it's done and push Cook button as needed.

3. When cake has cooked fully, flip bowl upside down and allow the cake to land on a plate. Heat remainder of frosting in your microwave for 20-25 seconds. Pour this frosting over top of cake and serve warm.

(6) Honey Ginger Porridge

You'll love adding fresh ginger to rice in your Japanese rice cooker, so your finished porridge will be infused with its sweet and spicy taste. If you add a bit of honey before you serve, it will balance the slight bite of ginger. This is a feel-good breakfast dish for anyone in the house.

Yield: 4 Servings

Preparation Time: 20 minutes

List of Ingredients:

- 4 tablespoons of honey, pure
- 5 cups of filtered water
- 1 cup of rice, short grain, washed
- 1 tablespoon of ginger, freshly grated
- 1 teaspoon of salt, kosher

MMMMMMMMMMMMMMMMMMMMMMMMMMMMMMMMMMMM

Methods:

1. Put water, washed rice, salt and ginger in bowl of your rice cooker. Combine gently by stirring. Set rice cooker for Porridge. When rice is done, open lid. Stir rice and loosen it.

2. Divide into rice bowls. Drizzle honey over porridge to serve.

(7) Rice Cooker Banana Pudding

If you've never used your rice cooker for anything other than rice, try this recipe. It's easy. Just check the cooker now & then, to be sure that your pudding is setting up nicely.

Yield: 1-2 Servings

Preparation Time: 90 minutes

List of Ingredients:

- 1 cup of flour, self-rising
- 2 tablespoons of milk, whole
- ½ teaspoons of cinnamon, ground
- 1 lightly whisked egg, medium
- 1 sliced banana + two extra mashed bananas
- 2 tablespoons of sugar, brown, + extra 1/3 cup
- 1 oz. of butter + 2 oz. extra

MMMMMMMMMMMMMMMMMMMMMMMMMMMMMMMMMMMMM

Methods:

1. Grease, then line base of rice cooker pan with parchment paper. Drizzle 1 ounce of melted butter on paper. Sprinkle 2 tablespoons brown sugar over top. Layer banana slices atop sugar. Set the pan aside.

2. Combine extra brown sugar and extra butter with cinnamon, milk, egg and extra mashed banana in mixing bowl. Sift in flour. Fold gently into banana mixture. Spoon over bananas in rice cooker pan.

3. Level top of mixture. Cover. Set rice cooker on Cook and allow to work for five minutes. Change cooker setting to Warm and allow it to work for 10 minutes. Set rice cooker back to Cook. Cook for three more minutes. Switch back to the Warm setting and allow it to stand for about 10 minutes more. Leave covered while doing these steps.

4. Repeat this process two more times. Toothpick in center should be cleaned when pulled out.

5. Turn pudding out onto a plate. Discard baking paper and serve.

(8) Poached Pears

Using apple cider, you can create poached and spiced pears that make a wonderful and welcome breakfast dish. You can even make them ahead of time – how easy is that?

Yield: 4 Servings

Preparation Time: 1 hour & 5 minutes

List of Ingredients:

- 1 x 1-inch piece of peeled, sliced ginger, fresh
- 3 cardamom pods, black
- 2 star anise
- 2 cloves, whole
- 1 clementine, peel only
- 1 cinnamon stick, 3 inches
- 2 cups of apple cider
- 2 cups of pomegranate juice
- 2 peeled, cored, halved pears

MMMMMMMMMMMMMMMMMMMMMMMMMMMMMMMMMMM

Methods:

1. Place ginger, cardamom pods, star anise, cloves, clementine peel, cinnamon stick, apple cider and pomegranate juice in the rice cooker. Place the pears in poaching liquid.

2. Close the rice cooker. Cook on the White Rice setting for 45 minutes. Mixture should be tender.

3. Open the cover. Turn the pears over and allow to sit for about an hour. Turn the pears again. Allow to sit for one more hour. Alternately, they can be placed in the refrigerator overnight. Serve.

(9) Rice Cooker Walnut Cake

This doesn't sound like a dessert that would lend itself well to a rice cooker, but it does. The sensors in rice cookers pay attention to temperature, as they are designed to know when a rice dish is done. It works just as well here.

Yield: 6 Servings

Preparation Time: 35 minutes

List of Ingredients:

- 1 tablespoon of sugar, maple
- ½ cup of walnuts
- 1 & ½ cup of water, filtered
- 2 cups of pancake mix

MMMMMMMMMMMMMMMMMMMMMMMMMMMMMMMMMMMMMMMM

Methods:

1. Combine water and pancake mix. Stir and eliminate most lumps. Add walnut. Stir again.

2. Pour mixture into a rice cooker. Sprinkle maple sugar over the top.

3. Use Sushi or Brown Rice setting to cook the cake. Top will not brown, but edges might. Test with a toothpick for doneness.

4. Turn out on rack. Plate and serve.

(10) Egg & Rice, Japanese Style

This traditional breakfast dish from Japan is basically just a large egg cracked over steamy rice. But it can also be splashed with soy sauce, or sprinkled with sesame seeds.

Yield: 1 Serving

Preparation Time: ½ hour

List of Ingredients:

- 1 egg, large
- 1 pc. of kombu (kelp), dried
- 2 cups of filtered water, + extra to rinse
- 1 & ½ cups of sushi rice, uncooked, washed
- Sesame seeds and soy sauce, as desired

MMMMMMMMMMMMMMMMMMMMMMMMMMMMMMMMMMMM

Methods:

1. Combine rice with kombu and water in rice cooker. Use package instructions to prepare rice.

2. Transfer a cup of steamed rice to serving bowl. Top with egg, sesame seeds and soy sauce. Serve.

(11) Mango Sticky Rice

This is such a popular dessert in Thailand, made with coconut milk and glutinous rice, and served up with slices of so-sweet mango. It can be made sugar free and gluten free, too, so it's healthier.

Yield: 2 Servings

Preparation Time: 35 minutes

List of Ingredients:

- 1 tablespoon of mung beans, toasted
- ½ teaspoons of flour, rice
- 1/3 teaspoons of salt, kosher
- 3 tablespoons of sugar, coconut
- Mangoes, sliced
- ½ cup of full fat coconut milk
- 1 cup of rice, sticky

MMMMMMMMMMMMMMMMMMMMMMMMMMMMMMMMMMMMM

Methods:

1. Steam the rice in cooker until it is soft.

2. As rice steams, heat salt, coconut milk and coconut sugar in sauce pan on med. heat until coconut sugar dissolves. Don't allow to boil.

3. Place steamed rice in bowl. Pour ¾ of coconut milk on top. Stir and then cover. Allow to sit for about 20 minutes.

4. Add ½ teaspoons of rice flour to the rest of coconut milk. Heat until it thickens.

5. Divide sticky rice into individual bowls. Top it with coconut milk thick sauce and then sprinkle with mung beans. Serve with sweet slices of mango.

(12) Rice Cooker Oatmeal

Using your rice cooker to make oats is easier than the "quick" method of overnight cooking, and you don't have to wait a whole night or think ahead. Just throw your oats and water in a rice cooker with a few pinches of sea salt, and you'll have tasty oats in less than a half hour.

Yield: 1 Serving

Preparation Time: 10-15 minutes

List of Ingredients:

- 3 parts of filtered water
- 1 part of oats
- 1 pinch salt for every cup of oats

MMMMMMMMMMMMMMMMMMMMMMMMMMMMMMMMMMMM

Methods:

1. Place water, salt and oats in the rice cooker. Cook up to about ½ maximum capacity, since the oats bubble more than rice does.

2. Press "On". Serve when done.

(13) Rice Cooker Fancy Chocolate Cake

This festive, enjoyable recipe combines chocolate baking powder, mini chocolate chips and chocolate syrup to create a wonderful cake that is sure to be a hit in your house.

Yield: 8 Servings

Preparation Time: 55 minutes

List of Ingredients:

- 4 eggs, large
- 1 cup of milk, whole
- 1 cup of oil, vegetable
- 1 tablespoon of baking powder
- 1 teaspoon of vanilla extract, pure
- 1 teaspoon of salt, kosher
- 1 cup of sugar, granulated
- 1 cup of cocoa powder, dark
- 2 cups of flour, all-purpose
- Chocolate chips, mini
- Syrup, chocolate

MMMMMMMMMMMMMMMMMMMMMMMMMMMMMMMMMMMM

Methods:

1. Combine the dry ingredients of baking powder, salt, sugar and flour in one bowl and the wet ingredients of vanilla extract, eggs and oil in another bowl.

2. Mix dry and wet mixtures together and add milk.

3. Divide this batter between two bowls. Add the cocoa powder only to one bowl.

4. Spread both mixtures in the middle of a cake pan, like you would with pancakes.

5. Turn on rice cooker and use it to cook the cakes. It usually takes about ½ hour, and sometimes a bit longer. Check with a toothpick to make sure it's done.

6. Remove cake from rice cooker and add chocolate syrup. Serve.

(14) Mirin Rice

This is quite a popular menu item in Japan. They use seasonal ingredients to mark the seasons changing. You can, too. Just add your chosen ingredients to the rice cooker and press Start.

Yield: 1-2 Servings

Preparation Time: 55 minutes

List of Ingredients:

- 2 shiitake mushrooms, dried
- Water to level 2 on rice cooker
- 2 cups of medium or short grain rice, white
- ¾ ounce of carrots, peeled
- 1/3 slice of fried tofu, chopped in strips
- 1 ounce of cubed chicken
- 1 tablespoon of mirin
- 1 tablespoon of soy sauce, light
- ¼ teaspoons of dashinomoto (Japanese soup base)
- 1/3 teaspoons of kosher salt

MMMMMMMMMMMMMMMMMMMMMMMMMMMMMMMMMM

Methods:

1. Mix dashinomoto, salt, mirin and soy sauce. Soak tofu and chicken in this mixture. Don't discard the soup stock.

2. Slice carrot into strips. Remove the hard tips from shiitake and slice into strips.

3. Add step 1 soup stock to shiitake water. Mix well.

4. Place rice in rice cooker pan. Pour in step 3 soup stock.

5. Add water to "2" mark on cooker for white rice or mixed rice. Combine.

6. Spread step 1 & 2 ingredients atop rice. Cook rice with White or Mixed setting.

7. When rice is done, open lid. Fluff rice and loosen. Serve.

(15) Black Bean Rice Cooker Chili

Chili has long been a staple in slow cooker recipes, but it works just as well in a rice cooker. The basic dish can be adapted easily if you want to use a different type of meat or beans. You can add some crushed red peppers in for an extra hot kick, too.

Yield: 6 Servings

Preparation Time: 1 hour and 20 minutes

List of Ingredients:

- 1 cup of broth, vegetable
- 1 large can tomatoes, chopped
- 1 can of black beans, refried, vegetarian
- 1 tablespoon of cumin, powdered
- 2 tablespoons of chili powder
- 3 cans of black beans – 2 of them drained
- 2 crushed garlic cloves
- ½ diced onion
- 2 sliced carrots
- 1 tablespoon of oil, olive
- 1 pinch sea salt, coarse
- To serve: chopped avocado and shredded cheese, cheddar

MMMMMMMMMMMMMMMMMMMMMMMMMMMMMMMMMM

Methods:

1. Sauté the onions in 1 tablespoon of olive oil in a pot on med. heat. Cook 'til they are translucent. Add garlic and carrots. Cook 'til carrots start softening. Transfer to the rice cooker pan.

2. Add the broth, chili powder, tomatoes and cumin. Set cooker to Quick Cook or Regular setting. After Quick Cook ends, or about 20 minutes later if on Regular, add black beans. Continue cooking.

3. When second cycle has been completed, add refried beans. Mix well.

4. Leave rice cooker on Warm. Serve with avocado and cheddar cheese.

(16) Rice Jambalaya

If you enjoy spicy food, Cajun dishes may be among your favorites. If you love dishes like jambalaya and gumbo, this may be a new favorite recipe. It's easy to make, since all the ingredients get tossed into a rice cooker, and there is little cleanup needed.

Yield: 4-5 Servings

Preparation Time: 1 hour & 45 minutes

List of Ingredients:

- 2 x 14.5-ounce cans of tomatoes, stewed
- 2 teaspoons of cayenne pepper
- 1 stick of butter, softened
- 2 teaspoons of garlic powder
- 1 teaspoon of chili powder
- 2 teaspoons of pepper, black
- 2 teaspoons of Cajun seasoning
- 1 chopped onion, large
- 4 cups of broth, chicken
- 2 & ½ cup of uncooked rice, short grain, washed
- 1 link of sliced sausage
- 1 chopped bell pepper, green

MMMMMMMMMMMMMMMMMMMMMMMMMMMMMMMMMMM

Methods:

1. Place vegetables and butter in rice cooker. Press the cook button.

2. After 10 minutes, butter should have melted and onions will have started turning opaque. Add sliced sausage. Cook for five to 10 more minutes.

3. Add remaining ingredients. Stir and turn rice cooker back on.

4. When timer has gone off, stir. Close lid and allow to simmer for 10 more minutes. Serve.

(17) Mushroom Chicken Dijon with Farro

This meal, made in your rice cooker, will steam your marinated chicken slowly on top of wheat hulls (farro). Farro is a slow-cooking grain that works wonderfully in a rice cooker.

Yield: 4 Servings

Preparation Time: 90 minutes

List of Ingredients:

- ¼ cup of parsley, minced
- 1 & ½ cups of vegetable broth, low sodium
- 1 cup of farro (hulled wheat)
- 8 ounces of quartered mushrooms, cremini
- 2 minced shallots
- 1 teaspoon of oil, olive
- 4 x 5-ounce chicken breasts, skinless, boneless

For marinade:

- 1 tablespoon of mustard, Dijon
- 1 teaspoon of oil, olive
- 1/3 cup of vinegar, balsamic
- 1 pinch each of salt & pepper

MMMMMMMMMMMMMMMMMMMMMMMMMMMMMMMMMMM

Methods:

1. To make marinade, combine those ingredients in zipper-lock plastic bag. Add the chicken and coat it completely. Seal the bag and leave in the refrigerator until you need it.

2. Set rice cooker to Regular. Place 1 teaspoon of oil in its bowl. Add shallots and stir to coat. Close lid. Cook for five minutes, and stir occasionally, until the shallots are soft.

3. Add the mushrooms. Cook for about eight additional minutes, 'til the mushrooms have softened. Stir in the farro. Cook and stir for about three minutes. Add broth and stir.

4. Place the chicken in rice cooker pot. Discard any marinade that is left over. Close. Set to Regular. Program will take one hour or so. Be sure chicken has no more pink left.

5. Place mushroom and farro mixture on plates. Top with chicken breasts. Sprinkle with the parsley. Serve.

(18) Ginger Chicken with Rice

Ginger recipes add a kick that will warm your belly. That's what

Yield: it different from teriyaki. This dish includes a balance of savory and sweet taste that is just so good. Serving ginger chicken on rice from your rice cooker is akin to what the Japanese call a casserole.

Yield: 4 Servings

Preparation Time: 65 minutes

List of Ingredients:

- 1 cup of coconut milk, unsweetened
- 3 cups of baby spinach, packed
- 1 x 2" piece of peeled and sliced ginger, fresh
- 1 & ¼ lbs. of cubed chicken, boneless and skinless
- 1 cup of rice, jasmine, washed
- ¾ cup of water, hot
- 1 large bouillon cube, chicken
- Salt, kosher

MMMMMMMMMMMMMMMMMMMMMMMMMMMMMMMMMMMM

Methods:

1. Dissolve bouillon in hot water in small-sized bowl. Combine chicken with ginger and rice in rice cooker. Arrange spinach on the top.

2. Pour bouillon broth and coconut milk into rice cooker. Season with salt lightly. Turn cooker to "On".

3. Mixture should be done when cooker shuts off. Allow to stand for about five minutes. Use a fork to fluff rice. Spoon it into bowls. Serve.

(19) Rice Cooker Veggie Frittata

This recipe will "sell" you on using your rice cooker for other dishes, if you're not already convinced that it's a great idea. It's a frittata that comes out intact after being cooked in your rice cooker. You can even use the bowl of the cooker as your mixing bowl. And, this frittata won't get crusty and brown on its outside like those made in the oven or on the stove top.

Yield: 2-4 Servings

Preparation Time: 40 minutes

List of Ingredients:

- 1 sliced zucchini, small
- 1 peeled & julienned potato, small
- 1 diced red pepper, small
- 1 peeled clove of garlic, whole
- 1 tablespoon of oil, olive
- Sea salt & ground pepper, as desired

For egg mixture:

- 2 tablespoons of cheddar cheese, grated
- 6 eggs, large
- 1 tablespoon of oil, olive
- 1/8 teaspoons each of sea salt & ground pepper

MMMMMMMMMMMMMMMMMMMMMMMMMMMMMMMMMM

Methods:

1. Heat a fry pan with olive oil. Add clove of garlic. Allow oil to heat until garlic has lightly browned. Discard clove of garlic.

2. Add veggies. Season as desired and set them aside.

3. Put a tablespoon of the olive oil in bowl of rice cooker. Spread around bottom and a bit up sides. Add cheese, eggs, salt & pepper. Beat eggs in bowl. Add veggies and combine well.

4. Put bowl in rice cooker. Turn on and set to regular rice. When this is finished, your meal is done. Serve.

(20) Mac'n Cheese

Who doesn't like macaroni and cheese? It's such a comfort food, for adults and kids alike. If you want homemade mac and cheese without the hassle, use your rice cooker. You may serve it more often when your rice cooker does all the work for you.

Yield: 4 Servings

Preparation Time: 55 minutes

List of Ingredients:

- 6 oz. of processed cheese product, cubed
- ¾ cup of cheddar cheese, shredded
- 1 x 12-oz. can of milk, evaporated
- 8 oz. of macaroni, elbow
- 1 teaspoon of salt, kosher
- ½ teaspoons of black pepper, ground
- ½ teaspoons of powdered mustard

MMMMMMMMMMMMMMMMMMMMMMMMMMMMMMMMMMMMM

Methods:

1. Combine 2 cups of water, along with salt and macaroni in rice cooker. Set on White rice setting. Cook 'til this cycle is nearly complete and most water has been absorbed.

2. Stir in black pepper, mustard, cheese product cubes and milk. Close lid and choose Warm setting.

3. Stir occasionally while you allow the macaroni to cook until milk is incorporated and cheese has melted. Serve.

(21) Japanese Rice Cooker Kamameshi Pilaf

This is a wonderful Japanese version of humble rice pilaf. When you let your rice cooker prepare it for you, all the ingredients will spend a few hours cooking in a tasty broth, which allows the rice to be infused with savory flavors. It's a nutritious main dish and works well for lunch or supper.

Yield: 5-6 Servings

Preparation Time: 1 hour & 25 minutes

List of Ingredients:

- 1 tablespoon of oil, olive
- 5 tablespoons of sake, cooking blend
- 1 teaspoon of sea salt, coarse
- 5 tablespoons of tsuyu soup base, concentrated
- ¾ ounce of walnuts, to top
- 3 & ½ ounces of chopped chestnuts with syrup
- 5 & 1/3 ounces of chopped green beans
- 1 sliced carrot, medium
- 5 & ½ ounces of chicken thigh meat, diced
- 1 teaspoon of sugar, granulated
- 2 shiitake mushrooms, dried
- 5 cups of water, filtered
- 1 & ¾ pound of rice, washed

MMMMMMMMMMMMMMMMMMMMMMMMMMMMMMMMMMMM

Methods:

1. Add mushrooms to rice in bowl. Soak for about 10 minutes.

2. Remove mushrooms. Add sugar and leave to sit for ½ hour. Then cover rice with plastic wrap.

3. Add water and rice to cooker. Add olive oil, cooking sake, salt and soup base. Add carrots and chicken. Re-add mushrooms. Turn rice cooker on.

4. As rice cooks, blanch green beans for several minutes in boiling water. Then run them under cold water, before setting them aside.

5. When rice is done, stir to combine ingredients. Top with green beans, walnuts and chestnuts with syrup. Serve.

(22) Ricotta Rice Cooker Gnocchi

Gnocchi are often misunderstood. They are basically soft Italian dumplings on a small scale, that hold up well to many flavors and sauces. You can supplement the taste by adding ricotta cheese, as I have in this recipe. Once you get the hang of shaping the little dumplings, it's an easy dish to make.

Yield: 2-3 Servings

Preparation Time: 1 hour & 10 minutes

List of Ingredients:

- 1 teaspoon of seasoning, Italian
- ¼ cup of grated cheese, Parmesan
- 1 egg, large
- 15 ounces of cheese, ricotta
- ½ teaspoons of salt, sea

MMMMMMMMMMMMMMMMMMMMMMMMMMMMMMMMMMM

Methods:

1. Mix ingredients and incorporate them. Refrigerate the resulting dough for ½ hour.

2. Fill inner pot of rice cooker 2/3 full of water. Set on Steam for 10 minutes. Allow water to boil while you are rolling the gnocchi.

3. Flour a cutting board. Spoon a tablespoons of dough on board. Roll until you form a small, oval-shaped dumpling. Set aside. Do the same with remaining dough. Add extra flour if you need it.

4. When cook time is counting down, add this gnocchi to water in rice cooker. Close lid. Allow to cook for about three minutes.

5. Open rice cooker carefully. Remove gnocchi that may have floated to top. Cook until remaining gnocchi have cooked. Serve with pasta sauce or herbs.

(23) Veggie Rice

This rice is flavored with sauces and vegetables of your choice. Making the choices is the hard part, since your rice cooker will do all the work for you. When you want a tasty, healthy, easy dish, this one will spring to mind. It will keep well in your refrigerator for a week or so.

Yield: 2-3 Servings

Preparation Time: 35 minutes

List of Ingredients:

- 3 sliced green onions
- ½ teaspoons of salt, kosher
- 1 & ½ tablespoons of mirin
- 2 tablespoons of sake
- 3 tablespoons of soy sauce, low sodium
- 8 cubed mushrooms, button
- 10 cubed green beans
- ½ chopped onion, small
- ¼ cup of shredded cabbage
- 1 peeled, sliced carrot
- 2 cups of washed rice, Japanese

MMMMMMMMMMMMMMMMMMMMMMMMMMMMMMMMMMMMMM

Methods:

1. Add salt, mirin, sake and soy sauce. Add water only up to measuring line in rice cooker pot.

2. Top with veggies except for green onions. Don't stir.

3. Close cooker lid. Set rice to regular/plain.

4. When rice is done, fluff gently. Serve in bowls topped with green onion slices.

(24) Rice Cooker Southwest Quinoa

You'll love using your rice cooker for quinoa. OK, so even though cooking quinoa on your stove top is easy, you still have to stand there, watch and stir it. A rice cooker can do that all for you. Just press Start and forget the stuff until it is time for dinner. The rice cooker not only cooks your quinoa, it will also keep it warm, until you're ready for it.

Yield: 5 Servings

Preparation Time: 1 hour and 15 minutes including 1 hour on brown rice setting in rice cooker

List of Ingredients:

- 1 cup of water, filtered
- 12 oz. of quinoa, boxed
- 1 x 10-oz. can of undrained tomatoes & green chili peppers
- 1 x 15-oz. can of rinsed, drained black beans
- ½ of small pkg. taco seasoning, dry

MMMMMMMMMMMMMMMMMMMMMMMMMMMMMMMMMMMM

Methods:

1. Mix taco seasoning, water, quinoa, tomatoes with peppers and black beans in rice cooker.

2. Cook on Brown rice setting, which will be an hour or so. Serve.

(25) Rice Cooker Salmon & Rice

This dish can be served as a side or a main, since it's filling and hearty. It

Yield: a great side with a salad or miso soup, for a healthy, light meal. You can even use the rice for making rice balls (also known as O-nigiri), which are wonderful for picnics and lunches.

Yield: 4-6 Servings

Preparation Time: 40 minutes

List of Ingredients:

- 2 diced green onions
- 1 & ½ cup of split shimeji mushrooms
- 1 teaspoon of fish stock, Japanese
- 2 tablespoons of soy sauce, low sodium
- 2 & ½ tablespoons of sake
- 2 pcs. salmon
- 3 & ½ cups of water, filtered
- 3 cups of rice, washed
- Sea salt, coarse

MMMMMMMMMMMMMMMMMMMMMMMMMMMMMMMMMMMMM

Methods:

1. Salt salmon a bit. Place on top of rice in cooker. Add mushrooms on top.

2. Add water, fish sauce, soy sauce and saki.

3. Cook in rice cooker until done. Leave cover on while cooking.

4. Remove from rice cooker. Mix and break up salmon. Top with the green onions. Serve.

(26) Tomato Rice

This dish is so simple, but so delicious. It is a lot like a pilaf, and your family will love it. You can make it soupy and wet to serve with fish, or creamier and firmer if you'd like serving it with chicken.

Yield: 4 Servings

Preparation Time: 55 minutes

List of Ingredients:

- 2 teaspoons of oil, olive
- 1 tomato, large
- 2 cups of rice, pre-washed, uncooked
- 2/3 teaspoons of salt, kosher
- ¼ teaspoons of black pepper, ground

MMMMMMMMMMMMMMMMMMMMMMMMMMMMMMMMMMMMMM

Methods:

1. Place rice in rice cooker pot. Add water to proper level, as indicated in pot.

2. Remove 5-6 tablespoons water from pot. Add olive oil, salt and pepper. Combine.

3. Place tomato, minus stem, in pot.

4. Place pot in rice cooker. Then cover. Press button and start.

5. When done, lightly toss rice and serve.

(27) Healthy Spinach Rice

This recipe is so simple, but so healthy. You can serve it with veggies of other colors like carrots or squash, or use it as an easy side for a meat main dish.

Yield: 3-4 Servings

Preparation Time: 50 minutes

List of Ingredients:

- 1 tablespoon of butter, melted
- 1 pound of chopped spinach, fresh
- 2 tablespoons of wheat germ
- ¾ cup of cheddar cheese, grated
- 2 cups of washed brown rice, cooked
- 2 tablespoons of parsley, chopped
- 2 beaten eggs, large
- ½ tsp of salt, kosher
- 1/8 teaspoons of pepper, ground

MMMMMMMMMMMMMMMMMMMMMMMMMMMMMMMMMMMMMM

Methods:

1. Combine the cheese and rice. In another bowl, combine the parsley and eggs with salt & pepper.

2. Add both mixtures to spinach. Mix butter and wheat germ. Spread on top.

3. Cook in rice cooker for ½ hour. Stir and serve.

(28) Rice Cooker Chicken Pineapple Fajitas

If you have a rice cooker, you can create this easy dish in an hour or so. Slow cookers are so slow, and rice cookers are so much speedier. If you don't have a lot of space in your kitchen, you'll be happy to have a small appliance that does so much work for you.

Yield: 4 Servings

Preparation Time: 1 hour and 15 minutes

List of Ingredients:

- 1 cup of water, filtered
- 1 tablespoon of tomato paste, fresh
- 2 garlic cloves, minced
- ½ onion, medium, sliced
- 1 cup of chunked pineapple
- 2 sliced bell peppers
- 1 lb. of chicken thighs or breasts
- ½ teaspoons of salt, coarse
- ¼ teaspoons each of black pepper, coriander, chili powder, paprika, oregano and cumin

For the spices:

- 1 can of black beans, cooked
- 1 teaspoon of pepper flakes, red
- 1 jalapeno, minced

To serve

- Feta cheese
- Cilantro
- Avocado
- Corn tortillas

MMMMMMMMMMMMMMMMMMMMMMMMMMMMMMMMMMMM

Methods:

1. Place garlic, peppers and onions in rice cooker. Top with pineapple chunks and chicken.

2. Mix spices, tomato paste and water together in small sized bowl. Pour the mixture into the rice cooker.

3. Close lid. Cook for 40 minutes. You may need to restart the rice cooker.

4. Check to be sure chicken is done. When it is, shred it. Set it aside.

5. Cook vegetables and sauce for 15-20 more minutes. Add beans.

6. Adjust seasonings if you desire. Serve.

(29) Vegan Curry Rice

Your rice cooker may soon be your favorite kitchen appliance. The work here is all done by the handy cooker, and the curry rice is a dairy-free, versatile recipe, with so much flavor to offer. It's a well-rounded, wholesome meal.

Yield: 1-2 Servings

Preparation Time: 35 minutes

List of Ingredients:

- 2/3 cup of carrots, diced
- 1 cup of potatoes, diced
- ½ cup of tofu, diced
- 5 bay leaves, dried
- 3 tablespoons of lemon grass
- 2 cups of water
- 1 & ¾ cups of white rice, washed, uncooked
- 1 tablespoon of oil, olive
- 3 tablespoons of powdered curry

MMMMMMMMMMMMMMMMMMMMMMMMMMMMMMMMMMMM

Methods:

1. Place washed rice in the pot of rice cooker. Add remaining ingredients and stir fully.

2. Place in the rice cooker. Use Soft setting.

3. After rice cooker is done, about ½ hour, remove rice. Serve.

(30) Thai Chicken Rice

This creamy, delicious Thai sauce has Chinese 5-spice seasoning, along with coconut and fresh ginger. What a wonderful combination! It's savory, and its taste may take your mind to a land that's far away and exotic.

Yield: 4 Servings

Preparation Time: 40 minutes

List of Ingredients:

- 1 sliced pepper, red
- 3 cups of rice, washed, uncooked
- 2 cubed breasts of chicken

For the sauce

- 1 can chunked pineapple with ¼ cup of their juice
- 1 can of milk, coconut
- ½ teaspoons of ginger, powdered
- 1 tablespoon of grated ginger, fresh
- 1 teaspoon of five spice powder, Chinese (available at most grocery stores and online)

MMMMMMMMMMMMMMMMMMMMMMMMMMMMMMMMMM

Methods:

1. Pour rice into cooker and add water as it indicates.

2. Cook cubed chicken with 1 tablespoon oil on med. heat in pan.

3. Cook the chicken until there is almost no pink remaining. Turn heat down to med-low.

4. Combine all sauce ingredients in separate bowl. Whisk to blend and remove clumps.

5. Pour the sauce over chicken. Add desired veggies. Cook for eight to 10 minutes.

6. When rice is done, scoop it into bowls. Pour sauce over top. Serve.

About the Author

A native of Indianapolis, Indiana, Valeria Ray found her passion for cooking while she was studying English Literature at Oakland City University. She decided to try a cooking course with her friends and the experience changed her forever. She enrolled at the Art Institute of Indiana which offered extensive courses in the culinary Arts. Once Ray dipped her toe in the cooking world, she never looked back.

When Valeria graduated, she worked in French restaurants in the Indianapolis area until she became the head chef at one of the 5-star establishments in the area. Valeria's attention to taste and visual detail caught the eye of a local business person who expressed an interest in publishing her recipes. Valeria began her secondary career authoring cookbooks and e-books which she tackled with as much talent and gusto as her first career. Her passion for food leaps off the page of her books which have colourful anecdotes and stunning pictures of dishes she has prepared herself.

Valeria Ray lives in Indianapolis with her husband of 15 years, Tom, her daughter, Isobel and their loveable Golden Retriever, Goldy. Valeria enjoys cooking special dishes in her large, comfortable kitchen where the family gets involved in preparing meals. This successful, dynamic chef is an inspiration to culinary students and novice cooks everywhere.

••••••••• ● ● ● ● ● ● ● ●•••••

Author's Afterthoughts

Thank you for Purchasing my book and taking the time to read it from front to back. I am always grateful when a reader chooses my work and I hope you enjoyed it!

With the vast selection available online, I am touched that you chose to be purchasing my work and take valuable time out of your life to read it. My hope is that you feel you made the right decision.

I very much would like to know what you thought of the book. Please take the time to write an honest and informative review on Amazon.com. Your experience and opinions will be of great benefit to me and those readers looking to make an informed choice.

With much thanks,

Valeria Ray

Printed in Great Britain
by Amazon

11640616R00048